One Wild and Precious Life:

Reflect, Dream and Create the Life You Were Meant to Live!

by

Nancy Dewar M.Ed. PCC

DORRANCE
PUBLISHING CO
EST. 1920
PITTSBURGH, PENNSYLVANIA 15238

Dorrance Publishing Co
585 Alpha Drive
Suite 103
Pittsburgh, PA 15238
Visit our website at *www.dorrancebookstore.com*

ISBN: 978-1-6376-4127-9
eISBN: 978-1-6376-4766-0

MY WHY!

Many of us are struggling to make meaning out of the lives we have been given. As we think about our purpose and what we want to leave this world with, it is often hard to figure out. This book is designed to help you reflect and gives you tools using an executive coaching model to work through and understand your why, your purpose and then tools to create a plan to make it happen. It took me years to find my why and here it is....

When I stand in front of a crowd of people that I have designed a training or keynote for and I see that what I say or how I say it actually makes an impact or causes them to think or do something differently, this is my why. It can also happen when I coach people, seeing them have an "A-HA" moment and then helping them make changes in their lives is very rewarding. Seeing people develop and move to a new and better situation is my why. Sometimes it's a very small change and sometimes it's life changing. My hope for you is that after reading this book you too will be able to write your why statement and create the life you have always wanted! This book is dedicated to my boys Nathan and Curtis who I have watched grow and become amazing humans, my dream for them is to create and live their best wild and precious lives. And to my husband Dave my amazing partner always supporting me to live mine.

INTRODUCTION

I love to see people thrive at what they do! I love to see people develop into their best selves. In the course of my career, I have worked with and coached many people to help them see themselves differently, to give them the confidence to be who they want to be and to empower them to live the life they were always meant to. For me there is no greater joy then to see this transformation and to know I had some small part in it, it is my WHY!

I have also been on a constant transformation; it took me a long time to figure out what I was good at, what excited me and then how to make a life and career out of that. I have been through many career trials, different jobs, companies, back to school and working through what I always hoped was going to be my why. I did not want a job; I wanted a career that reflected who I was and allowed me to do and be all the things I wanted to be. My family would say, "Are you changing jobs again?" I knew it was hard to understand but my purpose was gnawing at me and I could not ignore my gut, my anxiousness, my drive. It was constantly there pushing me to try something else in hopes it would fulfill me. But it never did. Not until I found work that complimented who I was as a person, that brought out my intuitive gifts, where I didn't need to be anyone but myself to be good at it, and what a feeling that is. It wasn't until I was in my 40s did this happen. I had many great years, successful years in jobs that I found unfulfilling. I left lucrative salaries to go back to school, teach at college, all in the vain of trying to find my IT my WHY. Now I look back and realize I had to go through all of those steps to get to the pinnacle, to truly understand what is needed and why and how I am good at it. Essentially, I always loved the people side of the business, training and coaching people and developing them to their next level, I never even tried to do that; it happened naturally for me. All I wanted to do was to have my team feel inspired to work with me and do great work, those things always made me feel worthwhile but they all came at a high price, many things about my job that I really didn't like to do or was good at. It wasn't until I started my own business intentionally to do coaching and training did I find true clarity in what I wanted to do and what I was good at. When large businesses hire you for your time to speak to their teams, ask you for your strategy or your coaching, it reinforces for you that you are finally in the right spot. This is not an easy journey and I know a lot of people are going through this or have gone through it. Some people never aspire to truly find their why and may settle, for some of us that is not enough and the push the drive or whatever that feeling is compels us to keep going. Sometimes your why is not a career, it can be family or volunteer work, there is no judgement it is all about you finding your fulfilling life. My goal in writing this book is to help you so that you don't have to wait as long as I did to find your IT or your WHY. I have learned over the years what tools and things can help bring this clarity to people. I want to share this with you, so that your journey can be shorter and fruitful, so that you can find purpose and personal success, whatever that is for you. I want to share tactics and shortcuts, ways to streamline your life into what you want it to be. I want you to live the life you were meant to.

My goal in this book is to inspire you to think differently, try some new things, reflect and assess where you are in your life and determine what is missing, then how to get it. I want to share what I have learned and empower you to move yourself, your mindset and your life to the next level. I want you to create the life that reflects YOU. All the best to you always. XO

HOW TO USE THIS BOOK: This book is designed to give you practical tools and tips throughout for you to reflect and evaluate as if you were working with an executive coach. It is filled with practical assessments so that you can start to evaluate some of the concepts discussed and where you may be on your journey. The goal is to help you self-identify where you are and where you want to be. At the end of each chapter there is an assessment on each topic so that by the end of the book, you can start to build your dream life and action plan. We start with *reflecting,* we then *dream* about what we may want, then we build a plan to *create* it.

Everyone is a genius, But if you judge a fish on its ability to climb a tree, it will live its whole life believing it is stupid. — Albert Einstein

CONTENTS

Reflect

Chapter One

DO YOU KNOW WHO YOU ARE?

Live Your Values, Work Your Why

There are some people who have a strong sense of who they are, what they like, why they like it or not, they have strong opinions, and show confidence in everything they do.

Clarity around who you are is essential as it is at the heart of everything you do, every decision you make and how you go through life. Without this understanding or clarity you are driving blind. Many of us are still grappling with a perception of ourselves that others have given us. It is hard to break free of the person your family thinks you are or your friends or your teachers. Over the years we are socialized by the people around us, the experiences we have and we come out of these situations with different ideas of who we are. When we do the work to understand who we are intrinsically and re-move the biases, we can truly find our best selves. This is not easy, but what I say to my coaching clients is that it's that little voice inside that if you are quiet you can hear what it is telling you. We have to do the work to get through the layers, to ask ourselves the tough questions and to trust our-selves. It took me a very long time to trust my voice. And I still struggle with this as others always want to put you in a box, that way they can control you or they think they can. Your power comes from disarming their perception of you when you stand up for your own thoughts and are confident in your own mind. So how do we get there? Working with a coach may not be something you can afford but it can be one of the best ways to help you to find your inner voice. You can also do things like journaling your thoughts at the end of your day, what went well and what would you have changed and why. The analysis of the decisions you made and why can help you see a pattern or trend that you want to change. Questioning the outcome and understanding who influenced this outcome if it was not you. Understanding what you have control over or not and determining if this situation happened again what would you do differently. You can also do some formal assessments to help you; some of these are quite reasonable and you can find them online. The one I like and recommend is the strengths finder 2.0; it can help you better understand your top 5 strengths. We want to use a strengths-based approach in our lives when deciding what to do and why. Remembering your innate strengths and who you are will help you build on these areas and make it easier for you to be successful and happy. The other very important thing is to understand your values. These are those guideposts that you use to make decisions and fundamentally help you best understand the life you want to live. Separating our values from our family or others may be difficult at first, as they may be tied so closely together that you may think they are yours. Separating our beliefs from those who are closest to us is a process but until we understand this, we really cannot be our true selves and build a life based on our why. Doing an exercise to identify your top 5 values will help you use these as your framework for all decisions and choices. If you have clarity on your value system this is your true north, you will know where you want to go and why and feel passionately about the choices as they are yours and yours alone. Sometimes we shy away from this as we may need to take a path that others do not understand. Judgment from others often causes us to question our beliefs or decisions and this may make us fall back into old routines or ruts. Clarity on your values and strengths should give you the confidence to build this resilience to move forward in the direction you are choosing. Sometimes those who love us question us at first but if they love you, they will learn to understand your why and respect your choices. Others may never understand and that's okay; everyone is dealing with their own insecurities and values and we have to respect that everyone has their own path to figure out. To help you determine your values you can use the below values assessment. Once we understand our values we can move to the next chapter in building the life you deserve.

If you are really unsure using more structured assessments can help. It can help open your mind to understanding what makes you tick, answering questions for yourself that you always had.

There are several different kinds of assessments, for personality there is DISC, Myers Briggs,, Hogan, and Predictive Index, to name a few. There are also EQ tests like EQi 2.0 to help you determine how emotionally intelligent you are. For more information on any of these assessments and what might be the best one for what you are looking to do, resources can be found at the back of the book. But for now, use this book as a resource and guide; you may be surprised on what you already know.

PERSONALITY STYLES

Below are four main personality styles. One of the keys to understanding yourself and others is to know who you are and then to know who you are dealing with. This can be used for personal and professional relationships. Social Style Theory is based on work originated by David Merrill, who used factor analysis to identify two scales, identified as *assertiveness* and *responsiveness*. This results in a model that has four quadrants, which identify four social styles.

The diagram has axes horizontally to represent Assertiveness (the way in which we influence the thoughts and actions of others) and vertically for Responsiveness (how we choose to show our feelings and emotions when communicating with others). On the Assertiveness axis there are two extremes of communication style. You either "Ask" people to do something or "Tell" them. In the same way, there are two communication styles for Responsiveness: Task Focused or Emotion or People Focused. When we bring Ask and Tell, Task and Emotion together, social styles are determined.

1. **Amiable**
2. **Analytical**
3. **Expressive**
4. **Driver**

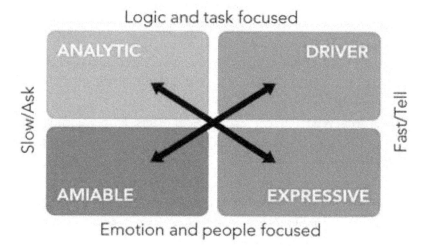

- The **driver** is a relatively fast-moving, logical thinker. Drivers need to be approached with the same style they possess themselves, although this cannot be competitive or confrontational, just logical and fast.
- The **analytical** type requires a somewhat more studied approach to matters, where issues are broken down into their logical components and methodically addressed.
- An **amiable** personality type is someone who moves somewhat more slowly and methodically; amiable types are more feeling-oriented, and require an appeal to their instincts and softer sides.
- The **expressive** type may require a somewhat faster, louder (or more emotional/instinctive), and communicative relationship.

Driver

Characteristics:
- Makes decision quickly, and with autonomy can be demanding, self-confident, enterprising

Typical Focus: is determining the best "business decision" quickly

Needs: Details, but in summary format to win, control, and succeed challenges

How to Deal with Them: Quickly and efficiently, focus on facts and details, use logical analysis

Questions to Ask:
- Do you focus on the task, talk about actions and results?
- Are you business-like and factual?
- Are you concise, precise and organized?
- Do you argue about facts, not feelings?
- Do you hate wasting time?
- Is your style of speaking fast paced?

Characteristics:
- Demanding, impatient, enterprising
- Result and/or task oriented (may neglect the people side)
- Self-confident, optimistic, positive
- May exhibit a lack of patience
- Needs to win, to control and to succeed.

Analytical
Characteristics:
- Cautious, efficient, meticulous
- Good planner, evaluates with logic

Typical Focus: Determining the solution that best meets the technical requirements

Needs: Maximum information, no time pressure, quality

Deal with Them: Give lots of information and documentation. Be very specific and provide space for analysis. Focus on facts and details. Use logical analysis.

Questions to Ask:
- Are you good with details?

- Do you take a systematic approach to solving problems?
- Do you love data?
- Do you like being the expert on the team?

Characteristics:
- Well-prepared, a good planner
- Evaluates and analyzes with logic
- Likes to see things in writing
- May get into "analysis paralysis" and miss timelines
- Needs to have all of the information, have autonomy.

Amiable

Characteristics:
- Patient, laid-back, considerate, friendly, emotional, and likes feeling useful

Typical Focus: Ensuring everyone is happy with the eventual decision/outcome

Needs: No stress or pressure; calmness
- To involve others in the process
- Time to allow the best decision to emerge

Deal with Them:
- Spend time/effort on rapport; build trust
- Offer to work as a team; go slowly
- Ask about their instincts
- Focus on what the decision makers will "want"

Questions to Ask:
- Are you good with people?
- Do you take time to get to know others?
- Do you work toward group alignment so that everyone is happy with the outcome?

- Do you work better in a team?

Characteristics:
- Patient, modest, considerate
- Intuitive and emotional
- Consults with others for decisions—great communicators, may not express own feelings if different from the group
- Likes feeling useful
- Needs to involve others in the process, lots of attention, time to allow the best decision to emerge.

Expressive

Characteristics:
- Emotional, outgoing, friendly; prefers teams
- Prefers change and variety

Typical Focus:
- Determining the best decision based on experience and intuition, quickly

Needs:
- To control the decision
- Public recognition and leadership
- No details; lots of summaries

Deal with Them:
- Builds rapport quickly and enthusiastically
- Simple explanations, few details
- Encourages trials and creative solutions
- Focuses on benefits to all stakeholders

Questions to Ask Yourself:
- Do you engage well with others?
- Do you take on extra work?

- Are you supportive of others in the team?
- Do you love to be centre of attention?
- Do you have a strong ability to motivate and inspire others?

QUESTIONS:

What type of Personality Style are you? If you are still unsure you can take the Social Styles assessment www.retaildoc.compersonality-quiz

How does this impact how you approach your life and work and relationships?

Make a list of the people in your life and identify their personality style and potential impact.

People in My Life	Personality Style	Impact
1. Partner	Driver	Provide details when making decisions
2. Parent		
3. Boss		
4. Colleague or Friend		

Are there any INSIGHTS from this section that you would like to remember?

1. _____

2. _____

3. _____

ARE YOU AN INTROVERT OR EXTROVERT?

Introverts typically get their energy from being by themselves, while **extroverts** get their energy by being around people. Do you like to network and meet new people, or would you rather deal with people more one on one? You can be an extroverted introvert, meaning you can be very social and like to be around people but too much of that will make you feel drained. Understanding what your first natural tendency is can help you to design your life so that you feel energized and create strategies to help you to be successful in some situations.

Although many people feel that introversion and extroversion are black and white, others believe that introversion and extroversion are two ends of a spectrum (people in the middle are often called "ambiverts"), or even that people can be extroverted in some areas and introverted in other areas.

Experts find in studies that the brains of extroverts and introverts really are different—it isn't just imaginary. Extroverts seem to respond better to social cues and rewards, while introverts are more motivated by ideas and internal rewards. On a brain level, it seems to be true that extroverts are more focused on the external world, and introverts on the internal world.

One way to tell whether you are an introvert or extrovert is often where you get your energy. If you get a lot of energy from being around others and being focused on people, but being alone drains you, then you are probably an extrovert. If you are drained by being around a lot of people, and get energy from "alone time," then you are probably an introvert.

Introversion and extroversion aren't descriptions of how shy you are, whether you can handle social situations, or whether you are a good employee or leader. Many people misunderstand this and think that being outgoing is a prerequisite for *leadership.* Both introverts and extroverts learn how to cope with the world, and can be great contributors and leaders. Taken from The Psychophysiological Basis of Introversion-Extraversion - *ScienceDirect*

Are You an INTROVERT OR AN EXTROVERT?

1. **Do you like to go to parties and meet new people? If yes, then you are an Extrovert.**
2. **Would you rather stay home and read a book or watch TV after a busy week or meet friends for drinks? If stay home, then you are an Introvert.**
3. **Do you often feel drained and tired after a day of interaction with people? If yes, then you are an Introvert.**
4. **Are you the person that knows the names of everyone in the office or your social circle and connects to others easily? If yes, then you are an Extrovert.**

If you have mixed answers or may say it depends on the situation, you are likely an Ambivert!

How can you take this knowledge forward to help you in determining your best life! How does understanding your needs to recharge help you, and how you can work around strategies to ensure you can be your best self when you are not in a situation that you want to be in? For example, for extroverts it is hard to stay home and not have social contact, for introverts they may need to do networking for their job and may need strategies to learn to do this well.

WHAT IS YOUR POWER?

Your Power is a combination of understanding your strengths and values and building around your derailers, aka opportunity areas. What sparks you to feel joy? Start with how do you build this into your life plan? The first step in any plan is self-reflection and self-awareness. Sometimes life's circumstances cause us to change our perception on things, but usually the core of who we are is still there and it can either help or hinder us if we do not build a life around the best part of ourselves. We need to listen to our internal voice to best understand our core foundation. Using our intuition and gut to help guide us and remembering to focus in on things that feel right. Paying attention to the nuances that literally in your gut make you feel different, good or bad, are the cues we need to help us identify our core selves. Our power is literally what makes us unique and different in the world. There is no one else that brings your energy, your talent and your voice to the world, only you. Each of us has a gift something to leave the world, something to make a difference no matter how big or small. When we think of a loved one who has passed and we talk about something they did or how we remember them, this is the best part of themselves, their power that we are referring to. It is the unique values, strengths and energy that everyone has and brings to their lives and others. I want you to tap into what yours is so that you can use it and build a life around it. Sometimes paying attention to feelings of jealousy or watching someone do something and feeling in your heart that you can do it better. Pay attention to those emotions, good and bad, what are they trying to teach you? When I think of my power, I would say that naturally some things came to me and for years I didn't pay attention. Finally, I was forced to reconcile the career I had with the lack of fulfillment because I wasn't listening to those cues. For me coaching and training naturally is apart of who I am, I don't know why and I can't explain it, only that it is very clear for me to help some-one get from point A to point B. How I have cultivated, my gift is the inter-esting part. I wanted to live a life with a career that brought me a lot of variety, flexibility, and was exciting; these were foundational for me and why I stayed doing work that ultimately didn't leave me as fulfilled as doing the work I do now. Some of my fundamental core strengths were not being utilized and therefore my power was not fully apparent. Finding a way to build all of those things into my life has been my life's challenge and why I ultimately wanted to write this book, to help you find your's faster. It took me a lifetime and I am still trying to get the balance right. I get bored easily and I move fast, but I also love to support and help others. So, I need a lot of variety in what I do, but the kind of work I do is very important. Having this kind of granular clarity is what I want for you after you finish working through this book.

For example, I started my career in sales. There were so many things I loved about being in sales: working with people, meeting targets, flexibility of working from home, travel and money. However, over time my need for greater fulfillment became clearer as there were many aspects of my job that drained me. Eventually I had to make a choice; I wanted to focus in on the things that I most cared about and was passionate about. I went back to school and got my Master of Education and became a certified coach. I slowly transformed my career into the learning and development space; it took time and was hard as I had to start at the bottom. The money and some of the things I enjoyed for my life like travel went away but eventually came back and then while I was doing work I was so passionate about. For some reason I had the courage to move and never stayed in organizations where I was not valued or fulfilled; I always looked for the next evolution of myself and my career. I believe each experience we have teaches us more about ourselves and through that experience we can start to create and carve our own reality. My mother would say, "How many jobs have you had now?" She could not understand why I was always trying new things and why I could never just be happy. I truly believe when we stop evolving, we start to die. The worst thing for me is feeling stuck; I have worked hard to educate myself to open as many doors as possible, and yes, I have moved around a lot, but I have met great people, experienced good and bad organizational cultures, and have learned what I am good at and why. It was all worth it! And why I want to help you find this for yourself!

Ways to Determine your POWER:
1. Strengths
2. Values
3. Derailers

Here is a list of strengths to chose from:

- Ambitious
- Authentic
- Caring
- Creative
- Dedicated
- Enthusiastic
- Flexible
- Honest
- Integrity
- Logical
- Motivated
- Optimistic
- Openminded
- Persistent
- Responsible
- Self-Controlled
- Trustworthy
- Versatile

What Are Your Top 5 Strengths.

1. Creative

2. Integrity

3. Honest

4. Versatile

5. Responsible

What Are the Things You Value Most?

Here is a list to chose from:

- Family
- Security
- Fulfillment
- Money
- Career Advancement
- Helping Others
- Being Loved
- Recognition
- Power
- Altruistic
- Security
- Privacy
- Self-Reliance
- Diversity
- Aesthetics
- Science
- Relationships
- Structure
- Analytics
- Freedom
- Flexibility
- Autonomy
- Fun
- Rile Clarity
- Cooperation
- Collaboration
- Modesty
- Intuition

My Top Values Are:

1. Self-Reliance

2. Freedom

3. _Modesty_

4. _Relationships / Family_

5. _Fulfillment_

What Are Some of Your Derailers?

Derailers are things you may not be especially good at or you know you don't like. For example, you may be a great salesperson but hate working with budgets and numbers. Or a derailer may be a quality you have that comes out under stress, like being impatient.

- Intense
- Moody
- Unpredictable
- Volatile
- Reserved
- Bold
- Stubborn
- Confrontational
- Ego Driven
- Dramatic
- Impractical
- Perfectionistic
- Micromanager
- Excitable
- Detailed
- Innovative
- Cynical
- Negative
- Distrustful
- Fault Finding
- Risk Averse
- Overly Cautious
- Fear of Failure
- Socially Withdrawn
- Entitled
- Arrogant
- Tough
- Uncommunicative
- Risk Taking
- Untrustworthy
- Attention Seeking
- Outgoing

Top Derailers:

1. _Perfectionistic_

2. _Fault Finding_

3. _Negative_

4. _Reserved_

5. _Detailed_

SUMMARY OF YOUR SELF-ASSESSMENT

Strengths	Values	Derailers	Insights
Motivation	Fulfillment	Important	- Need Variety - Need to feel connected to purpose

BEST AND WORST SELF-ASSESSMENT '

Write down what you are doing when you are your *BEST SELF* and what you are doing when you are your *WORST SELF*. Here is an example:

1. **Best self looks like this:** Happy, curious, open to change, nonjudgmental, focused, in good physical shape, eating well, balanced fulfilled career, and good social connections

2. **Worst self looks like this:** Lethargic, eating poorly, non-social, lazy, judgmental

Make a list of what you are doing when you are in your two personality modes. You can even add a picture to this list if it helps!

WHEN I AM MY BEST SELF I AM _____

active, eating Healthy,
fowsed, organized,

_____

_____

WHEN I AM MY WORST SELF I AM _____

Lazy, Tired, Disorganized,
eating & Drinking too much

_____

_____

Chapter Two

MINDSET AND RESILIENCE

Why It Matters and How to Use It

"Life doesn't get easier or more forgiving, we get stronger and more resilient." — **Steve Maraboli, Life, the Truth, and Being Free**

No matter what, life will always throw us curveballs; how we react to them is the only thing we have control over. When you are clear on your values and know the person you want to be, this can help remind us of how we want to show up. Our mindset is made up of our perceptions in life; what we have experienced to date will impact how we think and feel about the world. Understanding that you can have control over this perception and your own mind can give us the chance to make the changes we want in our lives. Mindset as defined by Carol Dweck in her book *Mindset:*

DEFINITION
In decision theory and general systems theory, a mindset is a set of assumptions, methods, or notations held by one or more people or groups of people. A mindset can also be due to a person's world view or philosophy of life.

By understanding that we tend to have two distinct ways of looking at the world, a fixed mindset is the belief that there is not much we can do to alter the outcomes, and a growth mindset that believes you can learn and grow and impact results. When you have a growth mindset, you look at a situation and think about all the ways you can make it better—what are the opportunities, what do I have control over?

Fixed mindsets tend to create a need for approval. "I've seen so many people with this one consuming goal of proving themselves in the classroom, in their careers, and in their relationships," Dweck explains in her book *Mindset*. "Every situation calls for a confirmation of their intelligence, personality, or character. Every situation is evaluated: Will I succeed or fail? Will I look smart or dumb? Will I be accepted or rejected? Will I feel like a winner or a loser?"

Growth mindsets, on the other hand, result in a hunger for learning. A desire to work hard and discover new things. To tackle challenges and grow as a person. When people with a growth mindset try and fail, they tend not to view it as a failure or disappointment. Instead, it is a learning experience that can lead to growth and change.

> A *growth mindset* refers to seeing your skills and abilities as malleable, where a fixed mindset assumes that your skills are set for life. Through putting in time and effort, a growth mindset allows you to *recognize your potential, build resilience*, and *approach challenges as opportunities*. – Carol Dweck, **Mindset**

Our mindset plays a critical role in how you cope with life's challenges. In school, a growth mindset can contribute to greater achievement and increased effort. When facing a problem such as trying to find a new job, people with growth mindsets show greater resilience. They are more likely to persevere in the face of setbacks while those with fixed mindsets are more liable to give up.

Which one are you? Understanding where you land can help you make changes in a different direction. It may change depending on the situation timing, so self-assessing can help you remember that a growth mindset will always help you.

Growth Mindset vs Fixed Mindset

1. Once we recognize where we are with our mindset, we can then take steps to improve.
2. It improves our focus, helps us make better grounded decisions and keeps us happier.
3. Helps us to manage our emotional intelligence. By having a greater sense of your mindset, you can then manage your emotions. Emotional maturity comes from eliminating the trigger reactions in the moment and this only comes when your mind is strong enough to control your outlook. Just like exercising our bodies to be strong, we can exercise and practice keeping our minds strong.
4. Helps us to build our resilience and as we move through our daily lives that are never perfect, we need resilience to help us cope.
5. Leaders, recognizing the mindset of your team and others can help guide the team differently.

MINDSET STRATEGIES

When you first wake up, take a few minutes to think about your day and what you want it to look like. Do something positive first thing; have a picture near your bed or in your kitchen that brings you joy. Maybe you use your favorite song as your alarm and it makes you feel good when you wake up, or maybe it's the smell of your coffee. Maybe you use a shampoo that smells great in the shower. Find the things that bring you joy and incorporate them into your morning routine; it helps to start the day off with positivity. When you have a tough meeting or a stressful day, use your music playlist to bring your spirits up and help you feel more confident and more like you.

Sight, sound and smell are positive influencers. Find ways to incorporate them.

Here are a few quick tips you can do in the moment:
1. **Practice awareness of your thoughts.**
   Recognize when you are having negative thoughts and replace them with positive ones.

   For example, if you feel like you are failing at a new task, **replace the word "failing" with "learning" instead**. Mindful meditation is also a great way of gaining better control over your thoughts and emotions and can help you transition from a fixed to a growth mindset.
2. **Be open to different strategies.**
   When approaching an obstacle, people with fixed mindsets tend to lean toward a one-size-fits-all solution. That's because they are viewing the problem in black-and-white terms. (*"I can either solve this problem, or I can't."*) Try different tactics and solutions until you find one that works well.
3. **Embrace your imperfections.**
   So much of a growth mindset stems from how you perceive failure and flaws. *See failures as learning experiences that ultimately pave the way to success* and recognize that imperfections are universal and can be improved.

By adopting these practices, you will notice a host of benefits.

Recognizing your potential to improve will help you **tackle issues with more ease, feel less shame and anxiety, generate better outcomes, and thrive in ways you might not have thought were even possible**.

Taken from Dweck's article: "Growth Mindset versus Fixed: Few Key Takeaways"

RESILIENCE DEFINITION

An ability to recover from or adjust easily to misfortune or change, Resilience means knowing how to cope despite setbacks, or barriers, or limited resources. Resilience is a measure of how much you want something and how much you are willing, and able, to overcome obstacles to get it. It has to do with your emotional strength.

How many of you have had challenging things happen to you? YET you're still here?

Two people can experience the same thing and the future results are different due to their strategies, mindset and predisposition. This is all you have control over. The more you experience trauma in your life, the more you have built up resilience strategies. These coping mechanisms are your tool kit to help you move forward when bad things happen. And whether you recognize them they are there, and we can continue to build them as we move through our lives. The COVID-19 situation has been a good example of this. Those people who were able to pivot and thrive had a growth mindset. The realization that there was only so much they could control and chose to focus in on the things they could change. Some saw this as an opportunity to open new businesses, to jump in and volunteer, to create PPE for those who needed it. While others coped with the strong resilience of understanding they had to just ride it out and enjoy the things in their lives that caused them joy. How we react to the things that happen to us defines our lives and the results of our lives. As we experience difficult times we are tested and it is not easy, but recognizing what you have control over and focusing in on these things will provide some sense of stability to build from. Also asking for help; this doesn't mean you are not taking accountability to solve your own issues, it means you are recognizing your limit on something and are reaching out as part of your growth mindset.

People go through different stages as they are faced with uncertainty and/or change. The below resilience model can help us understand what stage we may be in and/or others we are working or living with. Just like stages of grief, we work through different phases as we start to understand and cope.

RESILIENCE MODEL

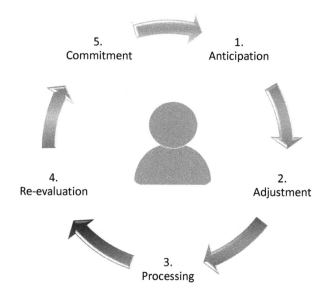

When faced with uncertainty, the first stage people go through is anticipation, fearing that things are changing or expecting things to happen. This stage is difficult as we do not know what is going to happen, and so we may start to overthink or worry about what we don't have control over. Once we do know what the change or situation is, we then start into the adjustment phase. In this phase we are letting go of the past and recognizing that things are different. If we use COVID-19 as an example, this would have been the stage where people were told to stay home and our work and social lives changed. We had to recognize that we didn't have control over what was happening in our world but we knew it was different. Then people move into processing and at this stage we know things are not the same, but we are not yet sure of how they will be. We may be starting to get some ideas of what is next but nothing is clear. In Re-evaluation you now have an idea of the new options, and you start to assess and evaluate what the possibilities could be. In Commitment you have spent the time in assessment and now are committing to the new normal; this is with a strong sense of the purpose. Once people get to this stage, they are on their way to a fresh start and have managed through and are now actively moving in a new direction. Sometimes we go through these stages over and over until the real end of a situation happens. For example, some people may have gone through layoffs as part of the COVID-19 crisis, and may have made it through the first round but then another round comes in. This propels them back into anticipation and the cycle starts again. It may be quicker this time, as they have just had a recent experience.

Reflect on the six items below and answer Yes or No:

1. When you are faced with a new problem, do you believe you can figure it out? Yes or No
2. When there is something that you need to learn to do your job like learn a new software system, does this overwhelm you or do you start to figure out when and how you can spend time learning it? Yes or No
3. When people give you feedback, do you automatically think of the negative implications or are you able to see what they are saying and learn from it? Yes or No
4. Do you think you are able to make changes to your life circumstances, or do you feel that your life course is pretty set for you? Yes or No
5. Do you think that others are controlling your life, or do you feel like you have control over your own decisions? Yes or No
6. Are you able to recognize when you are in a slump and work your way through it with strategies that you have used in the past? Yes or No

If you answered mostly yes to the above, you are in a growth mindset. We may not always have a growth mindset or it may take us time to come around to it, but if we mostly get to the positive thinking we are using a growth mindset. Sometimes we may need to challenge ourselves when we initially get stuck and move through a fixed mindset to get to the growth thinking and actions.

MEDITATION AND MINDSET

Some people find meditation very helpful when working on changing their mindset. There are several guided meditations that are available that you can follow along either in a video or audio format. By quieting the mind, we are able to get closer to our real feelings and better understand where we are at. Consistent work can actually change our brains to be more open and help us to manage our emotions and stresses differently. Mindfulness is also a great tool to use in your daily lives to help manage in the moment triggers. More on this in our next chapter.

Chapter Three
MINDFULNESS

Mindfulness is the practice of maintaining a non-judgemental state of heightened or complete awareness of one's thoughts, emotions or experiences on a moment-to-moment basis.

> **"The Awareness that arises from paying attention on purpose, in the present moment, non judgementally"—Jon Kabat-Zinn**

Jon Kabat-Zinn is the founding father of Mindfulness. He is Professor of Medicine Emeritus and creator of the Stress Reduction Clinic and the Center for Mindfulness in Medicine, Health Care, and Society at the University of Massachusetts Medical School. He was a student of Buddhist teachers such as Thich Nhat Hanh and Zen Master Seung Sahn and a founding member of Cambridge Zen Center. His practice of yoga and studies with Buddhist teachers led him to integrate their teachings with those of science. He teaches mindfulness, which he says can help people cope with stress, anxiety, pain, and illness. He created the stress-reduction program called Mindfulness-Based Stress Reduction (MBSR), which is offered by medical centers, hospitals, and health maintenance organizations.

One example of how mindfulness is being used is by physicians in hospitals and in private practice. Research has shown that mindfulness reduces physician burnout and medical error, reduces relapses in depression and has benefited many other medical conditions. There are many benefits of mindfulness.

Improved Mental Health
- Mental clarity
- Better decision making
- Reduces depression
- Substance abuse
- Eating disorders
- Relationship conflicts

Improved Physical Health
- Helps relieve stress
- Treats heart disease
- Lowers blood pressure
- Reduces chronic pain
- Improves sleep
- Alleviates gastrointestinal difficulties

Many people think that mindfulness is meditation when in fact meditation can sometimes be apart of mindfulness, but it is not mandatory. I personally struggle with meditating and have always found it challenging to fit this into my daily practice. Whereas I use mindfulness more like a tool kit to be pulled out and utilized when it is needed in the moment. A toolkit that you bring with you to meetings involving stressful situations, to any area of your life that you want to feel more in control of emotionally. I like to coach people around not having to sit on a yoga mat or adding anything more to your calendar but rather incorporating strategies into your life and routine that you are already doing.

I started to learn about mindfulness when my kids were getting older in their late teens and I began to realize that time was really passing by. I felt like I had missed so much and that the memories were blurry; sometimes I could only remember the moment from a picture or a story someone else told me. I didn't want that to be my experience for the rest of my life. I wanted to live fully in the moments, experience them and remember them. I was looking for a way to slow down my thoughts, be able to stop in the moment and pay attention to what was happening so I could really feel it and live it. Most of the time I just felt numb or anxious. So much is happening for us as mothers, who are working, worrying about your career, trying to manage a household, worrying about your kids. I created a life of chaos, doing a million things and never staying still. Being busy was a coping mechanism for all the anxiety and issues that I didn't want to face, but at the same time it stopped me from having true joy. Of course, I was generally happy but I had this uneasiness that I felt inside and when I finally realized that I needed to make it stop that time was really passing by and that I was missing out on the best days of my life, I wanted to make a change.

That change started when I visited a spa in Arizona called Miraval; they had a clinic there led by Dr. Andrew Weil, who had written books on mindfulness. You could take courses that would teach you how to meditate, and a very wise meditation teacher took me aside and relieved my anxiety about not knowing what to do during mediation as I could not stop my brain. They explained it needs to be whatever it is, take small steps, keep moving or listen to something to help you stay focused for small amounts of time. I worked on this for several years and finally realized that I could not do traditional mediations but I could train my brain to come back to the peaceful spot in my mind when I needed it. It became powerful for me to stop and refocus my attention to a place of calm even for a few minutes so that I could feel more in control. I could take in the moment, good or bad, and I could then remember it and feel it. Likewise, I recognized that I was managing many of the emotional things in my life by being triggered. Once I realized what triggered me, I could then create a strategy around these things. With the first step always bringing my mind to the calm, then being able to process and deal more rationally with my emotions. This led me to understand how emotional intelligence and mindfulness could work together and how to help others. I got certified in the EQ assessment and started to educate and work with others to help identify their trigger spots and how to manage the emotional areas that may be impacting their lives at work or at home.

Mindfulness takes practice and it took me many years to find the tactics and tricks that help me to get into the moment I need to reflect and move forward. Some of the things that work for me may not work for you, but you can keep trying to find ways to bring you back to your calm or feeling like you. I call this feeling centred or focused and calm. I can feel it in my whole body; it relaxes me and gives me time to reflect and it is the most wonderful feeling. Most times it does not last long, so I know that once I have it I need to use the time wisely. Sometimes I just take in the moment like when there is a family moment happening; other times I take a picture so I can remember the moment. Sometimes it is truly recognizing my emotions getting higher and being able to breathe and bring them back into focus.

Some of the strategies that I have used include the 5-minute breath; just take a deep breath and count to 5 and then determine how present you are in the current moment, with 1 being not very present and 5 being fully immersed in the moment. Rate yourself, then try to move yourself up the scale. Throughout the day you can challenge yourself to do this 5-point scale test, and the sheer focus on trying to determine will bring you up a number or two. It will also help you recognize what kind of things you want to control differently. If you are a 1 during meetings, how can you get rid of the distractions so you can focus better? Mindfulness has helped teams to focus better together. One strategy has been to leave your phones at the door in a pouch before a meeting starts, so everyone has their phones off and ready to focus in on the meeting at hand. Another simple strategy can be things like taking a walk at lunch, getting outside for some fresh air every day can refocus and literally change your brain. What you do when you wake up each morning can also help you with mindset and mindfulness; feeling happier can also help us feel more in control. Waking up to your favorite music or a picture that brings you joy can move your perspective into a more positive one right from the start and this can help you all day. A music playlist that makes you sing and reminds you of happy times can also shift your mood and your focus instantly. I remember using my music playlist when I was driving in the car to a stressful client meeting. It helped to relax me and feel more like myself and I always did better when I felt centred and more like me. Strategies do not need to be complex, simple but not always easy, and that is why the more you practice the better you get at it and can use it to your advantage.

Visualization can also be very powerful for people. If you are worried about something, using a picture of something that brings you joy or calm can help bring your blood pressure down, then you can think through how you may want to approach things. I know of many senior executives who have a picture of beach or their family on their desks and they use this to help them bring themselves back into focus throughout the day. Some of these things may not work for you, so you need to try a few things out and see what sticks.

Some of the more formal mindfulness strategies that I have used are a body scan; a full meditation would have you starting from your head and moving to your toes to see how each part of your body feels. This can help to relax us. Sometimes I just do one or two areas. For example, if I have been sitting all day, I think about how my legs are feeling and how to relax them and give them a break. Maybe I shake them out, maybe I get up and go for a walk—any body movement can help to make the brain flow and think differently. Sometimes it is just getting up for a cup of tea or some water, but during this time I am relaxing my mind and refocusing my thoughts and emotions. Sounds simple but it's not always easy. I can honestly tell you that after 7 years of trying out techniques and using them in the moment I feel more in control of my mind and my emotions.

You can change the prefrontal cortex with practice; you literally change your brain. The front of your brain is for the fight-or-flight reaction; by doing mindfulness you can increase the grey matter that allows you to control more of your emotions, less flight and fight. More in control and peaceful. It is not easy but worth it. I am experiencing my life differently. Do I still get triggered, yes, but it certainly is better than it was.

Here is a quick test to see how you are currently feeling regarding living in the moment and being reactive with your emotions.

1. When something happens, do you recognize your feelings toward the situation? Yes or No
2. Do you know when you are triggered? Where do you feel it, your gut, your head, what does it feel like? Yes or No
3. When you experience joy, can you relive the moment later in your mind and feel the feeling? Yes or No
4. Do you pay attention to how you react to something and evaluate the why? Yes or No

5. Are you able to stop, reflect and change what you might have said in a heated moment to something that you are proud of instead? Yes or No

6. Do you leverage emotional intelligence to help you navigate through your life? Yes or No

If you answered yes to most of these, you are self-aware and are living in the moment. If not there are ways you can become better at identifying your emotions and managing them. There are many books on mindfulness and emotional intelligence that can help or courses on mindfulness. Circle below your result from the above.

I AM MINDFUL AND SELF-AWARE

or

I WANT TO WORK FURTHER ON THIS

Chapter Four
PURPOSE

Purpose is the magical why behind what motivates and inspires us its our calling. Based in our values, our beliefs and the vision we have of ourselves and/or our lives. Purpose gives us the power to move forward in our own direction with confidence. Purpose creates our attitudes, beliefs and activities and constantly keeps us focused on our journey. It drives our motivations, our thoughts and how we show up. When your purpose is strong life is easier, as you do not second guess your opinions or thoughts; they guide you toward your end goal, effortlessly and easily.

Finding your purpose can be the hardest thing to figure out for yourself. In order to understand our purpose, we must first be listening to the voice in our heads that is trying to guide us, our intuition or gut feel or whatever you call it, it's there. Anything that excites you or lights up your heart is a good indication of what is important to you and what you care about. The things you are passionate about are not random; they are your calling. So, listen to them, explore them, understand them fully and don't let others tell you differently. So many times, people try to dampen our excitement about something because it is not theirs; they don't understand, nor do they need to. Feel the momentum in yourself in the power of your dreams when you are doing something that really makes you feel your best self.

My purpose was always there; I just needed to understand how to use it to fulfill my career and a life. What I want most for you is that you find your purpose and are able to make a life out of it, have it guide your career choices, who you marry, the person you are and the life you want to create for yourself. When we do not listen to what we care about or do the things we want to do, we have an anxiousness or restlessness inside ourselves that we may not be able to understand fully. It sits with us until we can figure out how to enable a life that allows us to use our gifts, our purpose and gain the fulfillment of doing what you were meant to do in this world. There are many ways to make a life out of purpose. For my parents, being able to send their children to school, help them with getting married and financially seeing them thrive in the world was their purpose. On their deathbed they said, "I saw everything, my children have homes, families, cars, they are successful people in the world." That was their purpose and for them it took a lot to do this, as financially it wasn't always easy. Pride in their purpose left them feeling that their life was well served and they felt content. Now you may say this is not purpose the way we may look at it today. We are striving for something very personal, deeper, a sense of ourselves in the world that indicates our special gifts in a way that demonstrates our uniqueness. At least for me that is how I would sum it up. My children are definitely my purpose and like my parents, this is at the core of my legacy and what I am proud to be a part of. But I also feel there is a personal legacy, who you are as a person, the gifts you bring that are uniquely yours to offer the world so you can feel deeply and personally fulfilled as you live your life daily.

There have been times in my life where I have felt this. And it is truly the best feeling you can ever feel. I don't want to take away from all the other amazing things that happen in your life, like the love of your children or spouse or family, but the personal individual feeling of doing what it is that you were meant to be doing. There is nothing stronger or more powerful than that, and I want each of you to experience a life filled with these moments. For your own personal fulfillment, to know you are truly doing what it is you were meant to do. When you think of doctors who save lives each day or figure out a unique diagnosis for a patient who has been suffering, these are very fulfilling things that happen to them as part of their purpose. Their reason for becoming a doctor. This can be true for all of us in our own unique ways. Once we understand what our it is, we can start to cultivate a life to build around it.

For me, I found my gift being on a stage, and this may sound funny but I truly feel more like myself when I am up in front of an audience being able to teach, guide and deliver on messages that make them think differently, learn new things, and connect with me on new ideas. I am my best self when I am able to help others to inspire thinking in a new direction. Guiding a room full of people, having them listen to what I am delivering and getting value from my messaging is truly my unique gift. As I started to pull away at this, it helped me to further develop what it was about this that was at the core of the fulfillment. For me it can be connecting either on a stage or through a coaching session or any way that I can help people understand deeper, feel more okay with how they are feeling, help them figure out their next steps, guide them to living their best lives. It is both the creation of the material that I am sharing as well as the connection with the people to make them move in a new way. To create the "A-HA" moments with them to see the shift and then support the change. Every day when I coach people, I see it, in their eyes, in their bodies, how they look at me with this curious lens of "How did you know that?" I don't know, my gift is to be very intuitive, wise and comfortable. People can tell me anything without feeling judged. This is what allows for transparent conversations that help people really understand the core of what needs to shift for them in their lives to make a difference. I remember the first time I coached a CEO; he was very much against coaching but had been coerced into doing it by his leadership team. I knew that I would need to capture his attention quickly and hook him in some way to get his interest. I remember the one question that he stopped, looked at me and said, "MMM, that is a great question." He paused for a long time and then opened up to tell me what was really going on and his fears. That is a breakthrough, not just for me but for him. I am sure he never thought this young girl could teach him anything. My power is to help you understand yours, how your thoughts and emotions can be your best advocate and how to use your intuition, your knowledge to change what is not working, to plan for a different way, get the resources you need to support the change or growth, to empower you to remember that you can do anything you really want to. And that you are worthy.

When we are trying to think about our purpose, sometimes we make it so hard on ourselves. Sometimes it was always there. For me, when I was in grade 8 I wrote a speech for a public speaking contest. I delivered that speech and won my school contest. Apparently, I would not let anyone else help me with the speech; it was my words and no one was allowed to make any changes. I then went on to win the next round and finally got to the national championships. My purpose, my passion, it was all right there in front of me at the age of 13. I wanted to inspire people with my insights, my ideas, and I wanted to deliver them in my way. Where did that come from, I have no idea. No one in my family did this, no one I knew of did. Many years later I am running training and leadership events, coaching and training people using my ideas to inspire others, and I love to be on a stage.

What from your childhood can you think back to that was innately there? What from the core of your personality can give you hints to what you are good at and how to cultivate it into determining your best life and your purpose? How do you use your innate gifts to build a life that is fulfilling and true to you as a person? Do the work to find out because it is so worth it.

To help people find their purpose, I usually walk them through a series of reflective exercises that can help them reconnect to their most inner thoughts and desires. People say it is hard to figure this out and it can be, but if you start to listen to the things that make your heart jump, excite you or elevate you, these are all clues to the things that your heart desires. Don't ignore or rationalize them, just recognize them and leave the sorting until later. Often the recognition of the signs needs to sit with us to help us build meaning around them. Why do I feel this way about a certain situation? Asking yourself these questions can help you with the underlying meaning or reasons. But we never want others' opinions or thoughts about what we love to influence us and unfortunately this happens more than we know. Our socialization can affect our mindset and our judgments, even with the things we know we love. It is hard to separate ourselves from the reality of the judgments sometimes, and so this becomes a challenge for us to let go and just listen to our inner voice.

Many times, if you go back to who you were before you were the age of 5, there were probably clues already being demonstrated. Or things you were interested in as a child or good at naturally before the world socialized you away from them. These can be powerful clues to your innate happiness and purpose. For me the story is so true, as per my public speaking contest. However, it took many years to get here because the socialization of being more and doing greater more important things with title and money became my focus. I was socialized to believe that material things were important and how people viewed you was the goal. I worked very hard for many years to achieve that, and then ironically this did give the me resources to now do what I really want to do, which is to write and educate. I always felt this anxiety or uneasiness inside because I wasn't fulfilled, but also I wasn't listening to what my gut was trying to say. This is partly my reason for writing this book, because I don't want anyone else to wait until they are in their 40s to start doing the work they were meant to do. If I had a coach when I was in my 20s, I think I would have had the courage to continue down my own path in a different way. Maybe not, but if I can inspire someone else to do that then I feel I have done my part.

Other ways to understand your purpose are to see how others in the world find theirs. There is an exercise called IKAGAI, which talks about how your passions and interests can combine to create life purpose. People who live in the blue zones in the world live longest and the most fulfilled lives. Their cultures and families are built on purposeful living, filled with the basics such as good nutrition and exercise and meditation. We can learn a lot from these blue areas—Costa Rica; Okinawa, Japan; Looma Linda, CA; and Sardinia—and how they go about their daily lives and why they live so long. See the exercise to help you fill in some of the dots.

IKAGAI MODEL

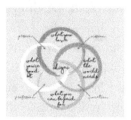

What do I love?	What am I good at?	What does the world need?	What can I be paid for?

Chapter Five
EMOTIONAL INTELLIGENCE

Emotional Intelligence is defined as:

> *Emotional intelligence (otherwise known as **emotional** quotient or **EQ**) is the ability to understand, use, and manage your own **emotions** in positive ways to relieve stress, communicate effectively, empathize with others, overcome challenges and defuse conflict.*

Understanding how your current emotions are hurting you or helping you is one of the most powerful insights you can have in your own behaviour and success. For young people starting out, having the self-awareness of how your emotions are impacting your relationships, your job and your overall life is a gift. It takes most people years of trial and error to learn behaviour that helps them to finally be emotionally aware and to use their emotions to help them. If you think of situations right now that trigger an emotion in you, whether it is anger, sadness or joy, how we react to these gives the world an idea of who we are. And if our reactions are not who we want to be, then we have the power to control those reactions. Once we are aware we can then control our behavior and reaction in any situation. This is one of the key things that no one teaches you; politically, emotional intelligence is one of the greatest indicators of success in organizations. Those who know how to manage their reactions and think through an answer in a heated moment as an example tend to get promoted faster and are deemed more likeable by the people around them.

Emotional Intelligence is now being used in hiring. In the past, IQ was the indicator of a successful candidate while now the combination of both IQ and EQ give more of a balanced view of a potential candidate. Emotionally intelligent people tend to be more well balanced, have more friends, get along with others and know how to navigate through their worlds successfully. Those who have a high IQ may be very academically smart but do not have the social skills needed to work in teams and be able to influence and work well with others. Working on your EQ can be a key differentiator for you as you navigate the work world and as you progress in your career.

There are 5 main subgroups and 15 factors that make up Emotional Intelligence as per the EQ-I 2.0 by Multi Health Systems, Inc. The five subgroups are:

1. **Self-Perception** - Made up of self-regard, self-actualization, and emotional self-awareness
2. **Self-Expression** - Made up of emotional expression, assertiveness and independence
3. **Interpersonal** - Interpersonal relationships, empathy, and social responsibility
4. **Decision Making** - Problem solving, reality testing and impulse control
5. **Stress Management** - Flexibility, stress tolerance and optimism

In the self-perception category this is how you see yourself in the world, your confidence, how you set goals for yourself, and how aware you are about how you show up in the world. The self-expression category is about how you express yourself through emotions, how assertive you are in your communication and how much you like to work alone or with others. The interpersonal category speaks to your relationships, how empathetic you are and also how much you feel you are part of a greater community or want to change the world. The decision-making category is about how you solve problems, how close your perception is to reality and how well you manage being impulsive. Stress management is just that, ability to tolerate stress and your optimism, as well as your flexibility around creative solutions to situations.

As you can see, there are so many key competencies that are required to help in particular leaders. If you think about the pandemic that we all went through, empathy and stress management were key indicators of businesses and leaders that were resilient through all the change and in most cases the ones who were able to pivot to stay successful. They would have needed to be very flexible with their thinking and optimistic to stay positive and strong when things seemed so uncertain. Emotionally intelligent people typically have the skills that can help them to cope with all of life's challenges.

EXERCISE: TEST OUT YOUR EQ READINESS

Think of a situation that triggers you, then write down your current reaction in the moment without judging yourself. Then write the reaction you prefer to have when this situation happens.

SITUATION	HOW I REACT NORMALLY	HOW I WANT TO REACT
1. COME HOME TO A MESS	YELL OR SCREAM	DEEP BREATH - ASK QUESTIONS
2.		
3.		
4.		
5.		

By strategically thinking through the way you want to react, your tendency will be to do it the way you prefer the next time it happens. If you take a quick second before you react, you will likely remember how you want to react and make the right choice. Our behaviour is our choice; the outcome of our behaviour is likely due to how we show up, how we handle our emotions and how we stay focused on exemplifying the person we want to be. Taking that moment to pause before we respond can be so powerful in getting the results we are looking for. Take a deep breath and count to 5, then respond. This can literally change your life.

Emotional Intelligence is something we are constantly working at and getting better at. Only CEOs who have been in their positions for very long time have an EQ that needs little work. That is because at that level they have learned to deal with it all, different personalities, situations, stress, and have successfully navigated their world. EQ can be assessed, and it can change with focus and work, so the good news is if you feel there may be some areas for you to get better at, identify what these are and how to manage your reaction differently in the future. Emotional Intelligence can give you the upper hand in life and at work.

Chapter Six

MOTIVATION

Why we need to understand what motivates us as a start to create our best life

"How we spend our days is of course how we spend our lives."—
Annie Dillard

We are born with innate likes and dislikes, our preferences make up who we are, what excites us, what makes us sad and what makes us envious. These emotions are key indicators and insights into our passions and our drives. To tap into these emotions can be the first step in really understanding who you are and who you want to be. Pay attention to your feelings; envy is a powerful emotion, one that can create some self-awareness into what you care about. Recognizing in yourself when something sparks you is vital to you understanding YOU. Dan Pink speaks about three main components of what helps us to determine what we do, why we chose to do it and how, in his book called *Drive*.

Autonomy, Purpose and Motivation combined create the inertia for you to move forward.

Purpose is the why, the driving factor that aligns you to creating priorities based on what brings meaning to you. When people lead purposeful lives, they are filled with a sense of focus, contentment, a feeling of satisfaction with where they are going and why. They genuinely seem happy. Figuring out one's purpose has been a difficult task for most; some lucky ones fall into it early and create their lives around it. If you did not know what this was early on, you may spend your whole life searching for this. Some people find it when they have children, as this is a powerful connector to not only themselves but to the sense of the greater good. The ability to leave a mark in the world through your children, a legacy, feeling like your life mattered for some reason. Others create this through their careers or volunteer work, some in their gardens; it is such a personal thing.

Most of us want to know that there is a purpose to our life, that our being here does matter and we want to live intentionally. The search for meaning matters but often we don't evaluate this until something happens, a death, an illness, etc. What if we determined this before something bad happened and incorporated it into our life plan, the life you are living now and making this your daily goal to create a well-intentioned life based on your purpose? Our wellbeing and quality of life depend on finding greater wholeness in life. Having a purpose in life, a clear reason to get up in the morning is essential to growing whole. - Richard J. Leider - *The Power of Purpose*

Purpose was revealed as the differentiator between those who reported living the good life and those not living the good life. 94% of those who felt their lives had purpose reported that they were living the good life and were happy.

When our work is not aligned with what we need and enjoy, problems in other areas of our lives are affected. The mental and physical cost of personal frustrations and stress can be high. Therefore, defining one's purpose may be difficult but in the end once found will likely bring the most happiness

Organizations are also clueing into the power of understanding their purpose and aligning their employees against sharing in it. This is different than a mission or value statement that we so often see on the walls in companies; this is deeper, an overarching reason that the company exists separate from just making money. People can better align their personal values with the company once there is a specific purpose identified for them to embrace. This makes people feel good about coming to work every day as it creates a different level of meaning, a larger picture, a chance to be a part of something great as people can align their personal values with the organizations. This creates engagement, employees wanting to work for the company because of all of the good they do in the world, or the overarching legacy the employees feel personally involved in creating.

The best examples of this are companies like Google, Apple and WestJet. What these companies do so well is define their brand alongside an impactful authentic goal that inspires employees to believe in the journey and be willing to bring their best selves to impact against it on a daily basis. One example is Tom's shoes; this company's motto is everyone deserves to not walk in bare feet. The CEO's mission to create the company came out of his life experience while in India, where many people he came to meet could not afford shoes and so they walked in bare feet. He could not comprehend this basic need not being met and so he decided to do something about it. He created shoes that not only are made of all recycled materials, but for every pair sold a pair is donated to someone without shoes. In order to align his employees around this mission, he held a "wear no shoes for a day" day each year, where every employee had to come to work and not wear shoes for the whole day. The response to this was overwhelming; the employees not only intuitively understood the value they were bringing to the world but then actually experienced what it was like to not have shoes. They are now personally motivated and engaged in this mission, passionate about helping the CEO meet his goal that it now becomes their own goal. Brilliant marketing and personally impactful for all involved.

Motivation is a funny thing; how many times have people tried to lose weight and don't? Let's face it, we all know what to do, but that doesn't mean we will do it. So what makes us do anything, what creates that spark inside you to make you focus on your goal and make it happen? There needs to be an internal conviction to the cause; you have to feel it inside you, you have to really want it. The analogy that most resonates with me with motivation is athletes; not only do they have specific goals they continually work toward but they have the undying motivation to keep going, every day, the conviction to stay on course, the internal determination and strength to make it happen. I am in awe of this power they have and the drive they possess to stay on course. Their conviction stems from purpose, individual and sometimes team, the sense that they are bigger than just themselves, and always inspiring to be better.

If you are working toward better understanding your purpose, there are many things you can try to help you identify this in yourself. As a start, ask yourself some basic questions as per the below and see where they lead you.

PURPOSE CHECKLIST
Yes or No

- Do I wake up most mornings and feel energized about the day ahead? Yes or No
- Do I have a deep energy a personal calling for my work? Yes or No
- Am I clear about how I measure my success as a person? Yes or No
- Do I use my inherent gifts or strengths to add value to my life or others' lives? Yes or No
- Am I experiencing true joy either in my work or in my home life? Yes or No
- Am I making a living doing mostly what I love to do? Yes or No
- Do I know what my innate strengths or gifts are, things that come naturally or easy for me? Yes or No

WRITE out in one sentence your purpose.

_____

_____

_____

AUTONOMY IS THE DESIRE TO DIRECT OUR OWN LIVES.
Autonomy is an important part of motivation, as you may not realize how much of this you personally value and how it will affect how you are motivated or not in your life. Autonomy leads us to greater engagement as we have more decision making over our tasks, time, techniques and teams.

Understanding how this affects you can help you determine the right kind of work for you. If you like independence and feeling empowered to achieve a goal on your own, then being a part of a team may not be the best route to go. If you are more of an independent thinker, you may need a job that allows you to set your own path, like an entrepreneur or someone in sales.

If you like being around people and being collaborative with ideas, then work that entails brainstorming or team support may be best. It is so important to think about what has brought you the most joy so far. If you loved group work in school, then a job that allows you to partner with others is likely the best for you. If you are passionate about people and insightful into their lives, then work that brings a sense of giving or caring may be for you. Autonomy is about the freedom to make a choice, daily, monthly or in the moment, on what you want to do without feeling constricted by anything or anyone.

AUTONOMY CHECKLIST
Yes or No

- I am able to work flexibly if I need to. Yes or No
- I am able to delegate tasks that do not allow me to use my strengths. Yes or No
- I feel empowered to do my job the best way I can think of and deliver on the results. Yes or No
- No one is constantly looking over my shoulder. Yes or No
- I feel like my boss trusts me. Yes or No
- I feel like I control my own destiny? Yes or No
- Others try to convince me to do things I don't want to do and I give in? Yes or No
- I listen to my own internal voice and follow my own lead? Yes or No

MASTERY - WORKING TOWARD SOMETHING THAT IS MEANINGFUL
Have you ever lost track of time doing something you love? It could be anything from painting to writing or spending time with your kids. This is called being in flow, and when we have these moments we tend to do our best work because we are so passionate about what we are doing; we are being the best we can be and forgetting about anything else. The highest most satisfying experiences in people's lives are when they are in flow. The relationship between what you have to do and what they are able to do is perfect; it is not too hard or too easy, and it allows us to just be present in the moment.

Ideally we find work that helps us to be in flow most of the time. Think of a professional athlete, a writer, a painter; these people experience this in their everyday work lives.

Also, mastery is about being clear on what your goals are so that you can work toward them and get feedback along the way. Without getting some direction on how you are doing against a goal, you will never really know where you stand on performing it.

MASTERY CHECKLIST
Yes or No

- Can you think of a time that you were so involved in what you were doing that you lost track of time? Yes or No
- If yes, what were you doing? Can this be something you build on in your life? Yes or No
- If you were in flow, can you remember what needed to be in place to create the right feeling to make you work your best? For example, if you think of a writer, sometimes they need a space that is quiet or maybe they get inspired by the outdoors. Do you have something that may trigger you to get into flow? Yes or No
- If you are able to first understand what your purpose is and then if you have some autonomy around how to achieve it, you will likely find yourself in flow and mastering the work that you do and therefore feel very fulfilled. This is the ultimate goal for people, whether it be in their personal or professional lives. To feel that satisfaction each day that you did something that was meaningful to you or the world. To wake up each day wanting to do more and always wanting to do better. Do you have moment like this now? Yes or No

If you have not been able to figure this out for yourself, then it is a good first step in understanding how to create the life that you were meant to live around your personal gifts and strengths so that you can be as fulfilled as you can. Motivation is a personal thing; no one can create this for you, it is your individual journey to understand it for yourself and to foster it within your world.

What were your top three takeaways from this chapter?

1. _____

2. _____

3. _____

Do you have a good understanding of what motivates you and how you can bring this into creating the next best life plan?

Dream

Chapter Seven
CREATING YOUR DREAM LIFE

What do you want your life to look like? If you had no restrictions and you could let go and dream the reality that you want, how does that feel? What are you doing each day, where are you living, what does your house look like, who are you with?

This picture you build for yourself when you let go and just dream can give you some insights into what is important to you. For example, my dream is to live somewhere warm, where I am active each day, hiking or walking, I am working remotely, writing and coaching, and I am with my family and have a community of friends close by to socialize with, my home is well organized and very open and has a bright feeling. This encapsulates all of the things that I value the most, freedom to exercise, sunshine to keep me happy, work that is fulfilling, family and friends to stay connected. I can actually visualize this reality for myself, and once we do this we can put into the universe our wishes, and research shows that this can be the first step in making it come true. It may not all come true in the way you actually saw it, but some of it may come true in a way that makes sense for you.

You can use a vision board to help you articulate what some of these things look like for you. Have it hanging in your room or where you work to remind you of the things that you are working toward. Each year I create a new vision board for what I want to get out of the year ahead. Sometimes I can't find the exact right picture so I just use words to describe what I want. I use it for my work specifically, as I may want to write a new book or facilitate globally in different countries. The process of sitting down and thinking through some of these images can help you work through the details and get clearer for yourself.

VISION BOARD EXAMPLE

Another exercise that can help you to dream the life you are looking for is using the coaching wheel. When I meet with a new client and they are not sure what area of their lives they want to focus in on, first we do this exercise that helps them to better understand where they are at in all areas of their lives. The activity is for you to rate yourself out of 10 in all of these areas and then determine which ones are maybe not where you want them to be and how to then create a plan to make them better. It can also help you recognize which areas you may value more than others, or maybe it's just at this particular stage that you are in why something is more or less important. Take a few moments to rate where you are on these pieces and then reflect on any insights or "A-HA"s you may have gathered from these.

COACHING WHEEL

What is your current satisfaction score for each area? (1-10)

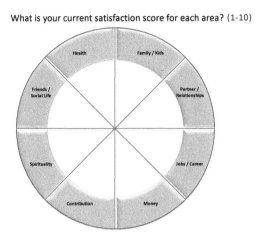

WHAT IS YOUR AHA?

AREA	SCORE
Health	
Family/Kids	
Partner/Relationship	
Job/Career	
Money	
Contribution to the World	
Spirituality	
Friends/Social Life	

After doing this exercise, what areas do you want to focus on more? Which ones do you want to do now and then later? How did this make you reflect on things that are not going well and what is important to you?

Another exercise that can be helpful is the eulogy exercise. Take 20 minutes and write your final eulogy. Don't overthink it, just write down what you want to be remembered for. Are you currently living this life? Are you doing the things you need to so that this will be your legacy? If not it may be a sign to make some changes and also can help you as you re-evaluate what is really important to you. Most people don't put a big house or a certain kind of car in their eulogy; it is really more about how they made people feel, what they did in their lives that made an impact. If you are not currently doing these things, how do you start to add them into your world? Were there any pieces in the coaching wheel that you identified that fit with creating some of these areas? The best part about doing the eulogy exercise now while you are alive is so that you can begin to live your legacy now. Don't wait until it's too late, because once we are gone it's too late. I started to write books because I wanted my legacy to be that I tried to put information into the world that would help people, at least to help them to think a bit differently and maybe inspire them to move in a new direction. That is my purpose based in my values, and this is what I hope these exercises can help you establish clearly for yourself.

EULOGY EXERCISE
Take 20 minutes and write what you want to be remembered for.

_____

_____

_____

_____

_____

_____

_____

_____

_____

_____

_____

_____

WHAT IS YOUR BIGGEST "A-HA"? WHAT DO YOU WANT TO CHANGE OR MAKE BETTER?

_____

_____

_____

_____

Other ways to help you to create your dream life is to go for a walk in nature and let your thoughts roll. Some people find journaling a good way to help you release and let go of things that may be hard to articulate out loud. When you journal try to not let any judgment into your writing, do not lift your pen, and just keep going. Even if there are spelling or grammar mistakes do not stop to correct them; let the writing just go. Many times when I do this exercise, it is literally me starting out with "I do not feel like writing today but I have to keep writing, so what should I write about?" Sounds funny, but set a timer for 5 minutes and begin to write without lifting your pen and see what you get! I bet something of value will come to light!

MY DREAM IS...

_____

_____

_____

_____

Allowing ourselves to dream keeps us feeling hopeful and in control of our destiny. Once we get clear on some of the things that matter to us, the next step is then to identify any barriers or things that will cause you to not be able to make it happen. Once you determine these you can then look at ways around it, and maybe in the short term it is not feasible but maybe as a longer-term goal you can work toward this. If something is truly important to you, I believe you will make it come true.

WRITE DOWN ANY BARRIERS OR OBSTACLES YOU FORESEE IN STOPPING YOU FROM GETTING YOUR DREAMS

OBSTACLE	WHY	WHAT CAN I DO TO MAKE IT BETTER

Chapter Eight

FINDING WORK THAT SUITS YOU

Culture, personality, drive, strengths and power

Now that you have done some work on who you are, what motivates you and what kind of life you would like to create for yourself, you can now piece together what kind of work you want to be doing. Whether you are a new grad or been in the workforce for a while and are looking to make a change all of the things we have been exploring in this book, it should be helping you to craft your ideal type of work.

Leaning in on strengths as your first area to consider, I always believe that if we build a life based on what we are good at innately, then life will be easier. We spend a lot of time focusing in on things that need to be improved versus cultivating our natural gifts. Can you imagine if we tried to get the best painters of our time to be better at doing their administration versus spending the time crafting their originals? Although it is good to work on things that may be a barrier for us, we also need to ensure the ratio of things we are good at versus not are in our favor. My experience has taught me that too many managers focus in on areas of employees' performance based on what they need to improve or get better. What if we recognized our employees for their strengths and focused their roles and time on opening up ways for them to be more successful? It is a mindset shift for leaders, and obviously the basics need to be in place and people in roles where they have some fundamental skillsets already. What I mean is someone who is a natural people person shouldn't be trying to be a numbers person and spending a lot of time working on something that would take them years to be good at. We need both people people and numbers people, and as long as you can manage enough with numbers that it doesn't inhibit your life, then spending more time on it isn't what your life should be about.

I had a fundamental shift during my career. I was in sales and loved many parts of my role. Particularly coaching and training other salespeople and being a sales manager. I also liked dealing with my customers and hitting targets. What I didn't love was the business analytics that came along with the role and the increasing administrative tasks that companies were wanting from this role. Could I do the analytics and admin, yes, but it was so draining for me and took so much of my energy that I didn't have a lot left to do the things I was good at and needed to do to progress my team. I finally came to know that I wanted to shift my career, so I went back to school to get my Masters of Education, as I wanted to be seen as credible in the space of training and development. It took many years to make this shift, and even after I became a certified coach and worked in learning and development for many years people still saw me as a salesperson. Good companies and leaders would take advantage of the skillsets I have with both the sales ability and the learning and development background. Eventually I did find a consulting role that utilized all of my areas of strength and that is when I was thriving in my work. I would sell in and then create and execute learning and coaching programs. I was able to use all of my strengths and experience in a way that I could build the business but also be personally fulfilled. This took years for me to accomplish and find. Many tries at new and different companies and roles. Some very good leaders and some not so much, but all taught me who I wanted to be as a leader and what kind of company I wanted to work for.

The other thing that I learned through all of this trial-and-error is about culture in an organization. Every company you work for has a different way you feel when you work there. Company culture makes a huge difference in employee satisfaction because even when I was doing great work for my clients, there were times that the company I worked for didn't share my values and outlook. It is difficult to work or lead in a company that doesn't recognize the things you see as important, and therefore lots of conflict comes from not seeing eye to eye on things. Of course, the company leadership is always what you need to follow as long as you are at that company, but recognizing where those difference may be and what kind of culture may work for you is an important piece when considering the kind of work to do as well as where to work.

> *ORGANIZATIONAL CULTURE is defined as the values and behaviours that contribute to the unique social and psychological environment of a business.*

When you talk to employees about the company they work for, ask, how does it feel to work there? Are you empowered, motivated, feel inspired toward the company goals? Is there career development, do they seem to care about you as a person? Is the company forward thinking and well planned for success? When the right things are in place and there is the right leadership, employees will want to work for the company. Their employee experience is positive and well aligned with their individual values and goals. They will feel like their own goals and fulfillment can be met while working for this company. Also the kind of people who are already working there can give you an idea of who fits into the culture. Getting the right fit in an organization is as important as having the right skillset for overall happiness and success in a role.

When you are considering what type of work to do thinking about the kind of organization you want to work for is also key. Think about your personality style. Do you like to be a part of a team, would you rather work alone, do you like flexibility or more routine, do you prefer a fast pace or more of a regular cadence to your work? Do you need a lot of change or prefer to know what is required and can be more planful of work activities? These are important questions to ask yourself as you are starting to plan for the kind of future that will really help you feel motivated and happy.

Chapter Nine
LEADERSHIP

Being the Leader in Your Own Life

"Your life is your own, you mold it, you make it."
– Eleanor Roosevelt

Why would I include a chapter on leadership in this book about YOU?

Because half of being happy with your work is finding the right environment and the right leadership.

Having leaders who are visionary, smart but supportive can make all of the difference for your happiness. Leaders who know how to inspire you to the next level while still being able to push you further when you are stuck. Great leaders are hard to come by, and this skill is becoming more and more absent in large teams of executives who are responsible for the bottom line. It is important to understand what kind of leader you would work best with. Organizations struggle with hiring competent people to fill leadership roles, competent in their core area of focus but then also in the skill of leadership.

What makes a good leader? According to John Maxwell, a good leader is:

"Being a great leader is all about having a genuine willingness and a true commitment to lead others to achieve a common vision and goals through positive influence. No leader can ever achieve anything great or long-lasting all alone. Teamwork goes hand in hand with leadership. Leadership is about people—and for people" (June 5, 2015).

In my experience a good leader is one who knows your strengths and utilizes you for those, one who inspires you to get better and provides a path or vision of how to get there. A leader is someone who isn't afraid to have their own vision, to push boundaries, to make changes when necessary and who you know will always have your back.

Children are rewarded for compliance, not for independent thinking or creativity. If you follow the rules and do as you are told you are good, if you follow your heart and express yourself outside the norm, you are unruly. How many young children have suffered this fate over the years in schools where teachers punish their enthusiasm, make them sit when they need to move to be productive, discipline them for not being quiet and listening? What a shame that we have squashed the innate passions and drives of these young people who ultimately have the potential to grow up to be the next leader of the world.

We should be fostering their autonomy, their confidence in being themselves and speaking their minds. Instead they are judged and shamed into getting in line.

Managers versus leaders: Managers are task oriented and usually performance driven, leaders are more big picture and tend to be more visionary. Leaders set the stage for possibility and inspire those around them to do better, different, more. A leader is contagious, not always the favorite as they are not afraid to go their own path but always seeing the world in a new way.

Brene Brown defines leadership as:

> *I define a leader as anyone who takes responsibility for finding the potential in people and processes, and who has the courage to develop that potential. The courage to be vulnerable is not about winning or losing, it's about the courage to show up when you can't predict or control the outcome"* *(Aug. 1, 2019).*

It is important that you become the leader of your life. Only you can chart the course based on your vision and what feels right to you. Even if you are not sure what the path is, it is important to keep asking yourself the questions of clarity. "Daily decisions determines destiny." Choices you make daily, whether you realize it or not, guide and direct your future. It is crucial to get clarity on where you want to end up so you can keep your compass heading in the right direction. Time is not always on your side, so don't keep thinking one day I will be where I want or assume that time will automatically present you with your goals at the end. The time to make your life yours is now; the sooner you take control, the more satisfied you will be with your outcome. You need to direct your actions toward your end goal and then slowly watch as things come together. No one had it figured out; even those we admire had to test new things out and see what stuck as they went. No one had a life plan all carved out for them; most took chances by listening to what felt right and if it didn't work they moved on to something new. The most important thing is to continue to focus on things that you like and inspire you. Maybe you love animals and you have gone to school for accounting, then maybe you can get a job in a business that helps animals as a start and see where your heart leads you. And so keep trying; this is being the leader in your own life. Many times I was questioned on why I wanted to make a change or what I didn't like about my current job; I was always evaluating where I was. I had an end goal but I wasn't sure what it really looked like or how to get there. Being a leader in your own life means listening to your own gut and making decisions and changes that feel right. Sometimes you can't even explain why, only that it is something that interests you at the time. I had a hard time staying in a job or with a company that wasn't supporting my personal goals or helping to develop me in some way. I was spoiled working for a company when I first got out of school that had great leadership. Right from the start I knew they saw me for who I was and what I could bring; they encouraged me to try new things, and when I expressed areas that I wanted to be a part of the opportunities were created for me. That was great leadership, leaders listening to the needs of their employees supporting their interests as well as the company's. These leaders also empowered and held me accountable for my role; I felt like people believed in me and always had my back. Once I left this organization to get new experience, I never really found the same kind of leadership. They had given me such a solid base to understand what good leadership is, what it looks like and how it feels.

Great leaders do the following:
1. Listen intently
2. Coach with a slant on motivation, always knowing how to lift you up while giving you direction
3. Have a plan for you, a vision they see, what you need to do to get better and help you to understand your own plan and create the next steps
4. Recognize and reward for work you have done, real authentic recognition; this means that sometimes it comes in words only but always followed up financially and/or also with promotion or next-step opportunities
5. Make you feel like you and your contribution are an important part of the success of the company
6. Let you make mistakes and learn from them without getting beat up
7. Have a vision for the company and where things are headed so you can buy into the WHY and understand how you fit into the big picture
8. Great leaders are not all about themselves; they see themselves as part of the team and supporting each other
9. They will admit to mistakes and ask for suggestions
10. Will not hold you back from your next role but encourage you to do the right next thing for you.

MENTORSHIP

Finding a good mentor for yourself can be key in helping you learn how to be a great leader of yourself and of others. Find someone whose values are aligned with your own. There are many great leaders who want to help and motivate the next generation, who want to help them to continue to dream and aspire for all the things you want out of your life. Mentors can be chosen for different reasons, different things you are currently needing. For example, if you are a mid-level executive looking for your next promotion, then you need to find the mentor who has that kind of experience "been there, done that." If you are looking for help in a particular career area, maybe you want to become an engineer and want to ensure you are doing everything you need to get there. You can join mentor programs who can set you up with a mentor and usually have regular meetings and conferences that you can be a part of.

LEADERSHIP AND EMOTIONAL INTELLIGENCE

We already touched on EQ and one of the most powerful uses of EQ competency is for leaders. Leadership and emotional intelligence should be taught in schools; these two elements are the most powerful way to model your own life and will help you guide yourself into your best life. Emotional intelligence is understanding how you use your emotions to help you manage yourself, your team, and your life. Those who have been in the working world a long time have learned ways around situations to work better and more positively through areas of conflict. When hiring for jobs, companies used to look for a certain IQ number only; now good organizations look to assess the EQ number as well. Someone who is well balanced between both IQ and EQ will be more successful in any role. Emotional intelligence comes from understanding what makes you tick, what upsets you and how you are likely to react in a certain situation. By understanding these things, you can then choose how you want to respond. What brand you want to be creating in your work and your life; this comes from self-control on your behavior and actions. Self-awareness and empathy are two areas of EQ that are powerful conduits to creating your own way in the world. The areas of EQ are the following (taken from the EQ-1 2.0 MHS): Great leaders have a high self-awareness; they are always trying to get better and work at being the best role models for their teams.

TAKE THE BELOW QUICK EQ TEST TO DETERMINE IF YOU ARE AN EMOTIONALLY INTELLIGENT LEADER AND HOW IT MAY BE HELPING YOU OR HURTING YOU.

(1 being not so much, 3 neutral, and 4 or 5 being yes)

1. I often self-evaluate where I am on my goals.
   1   2   3   4   5
2. I usually feel optimistic about making a change in my future.
   1   2   3   4   5

3. When I set my mind to things, I usually get them done.
    1   2   3   4   5
4. I am able to express my thoughts and feelings and people listen.
    1   2   3   4   5
5. I think before I act.
    1   2   3   4   5
6. I can make a decision in a timely fashion.
    1   2   3   4   5
7. I listen and can understand how others feel.
    1   2   3   4   5
8. I am patient.
    1   2   3   4   5
9. I can handle stressful situations.
    1   2   3   4   5
10. I know how to destress and have strategies in place to help to do this.
    1   2   3   4   5

If you answered more than 6 at 4 or 5, you are using your emotional intelligence to help you be a good leader in your life. If not, look at the areas you scored lower on and try to think of some examples of how this may be impacting you and what you may want to change.

Things do not always come out exactly as you imagined them, and sometimes you get what you need. But having faith in the future will only help you get as close to your dreams as you can. Feeling optimistic and listening to what feels right to us is a courageous and wonderful way to guide your life. Be the leader you want to see in the world!!!

Chapter Ten

WHAT DOES ORGANIZATIONAL CULTURE HAVE TO DO WITH ANYTHING?

Every workplace has a specific culture that impacts how people feel about going to work each day. Culture is a hard thing to put a definition to as it is something you feel, you experience, you just know. Employees try to articulate it and sometimes it is difficult to really explain in words. It is the pulse of the organization; it is what feeds or drains the activity, it is what makes you either want to be there or not.

An **organization's culture** defines the proper way to behave within the **organization**. This **culture** consists of shared beliefs and values established by leaders and then communicated and reinforced through various methods, ultimately shaping employee perceptions, behaviors and understanding. It is how it feels to work there.

Why would I talk about this topic in a book **about building an authentic life for YOU?**

It is because no one ever makes the connection for you. Until I started working in different companies, I never understood how much this could impact me. Until I worked in an environment with a poor culture did I realize what a good one looked like. The culture of the organization is a very important factor when you are deciding what kind of work to do and where you want to work. Being able to assess this ahead of making any employment decision is a key strategy for future happiness. At the end of this chapter I will provide a few questions to ask the hiring manager and people who are already working in the organization when you are going through the interview process.

Culture is one of the key components of FIT. Fitting into the group that you work with each day is like fitting into your social circle. You have shared interests, common goals, similar skillsets and similar outlooks on life. Getting a sense of what this is ahead of time can help you make a better decision of what type of place you may want to work in or not.

If you were to work in a marketing or advertising agency, you typically would have been drawn to this type of work because you were creative, more free spirited, like to do a lot of different types of things in a workday and like to work with teams of people. So you can imagine the type of environment a marketing or advertising agency may have. The environment is fun, fast paced, more relaxed, people wear jeans to work and don't work in structured offices. They tend to work in large group spaces and have flexible hours.

To the other extreme, if you were really good with numbers and took accounting, the environment would likely reflect a more structured tone, a lot of offices with closed doors, a very quiet place to work with people's heads down on tasks and not a lot of collaboration or teamwork. People may be social but save that for lunch or after work.

Neither is either good or bad; it is all about preference. These, of course, are very basic generalizations, and each profession and company can be many layers of these examples. But still important as to why you need to understand who you are before you choose what kind of environment to work in.

I can speak from experience on this one. When I was in university getting my business degree, I was lucky enough to get an office job for the summer in an accounting office. When I finished my degree, the only work I could get was in accounting since I had experience in that area. My first real job was in an accounting office Downtown Toronto for a large corporate organization.

I was just happy to have a job and didn't even think about the kind of work I was doing or the culture. Well, what an interesting experiment this was. I would go to work each day excited about my new job and the new friends I would make. Only to be disappointed when no one noticed or commented, no one wanted to chat, everyone just wanted to work heads down. They were not rude or mean, they just wanted to get their work done without any conversation or idle chitchat. After three months my boss kindly took me aside and said, "Nancy, we all really like you, you have been a ray of sunshine in our department; however, I think you may be happier in a marketing or HR position, where you deal more with people." "A-HA, yes, I would love that!" I said. "How do we make this happen?" And there was a sign of things to come; trying to get the right fit for who I was authentically as a person was where I needed to focus and find the right fit. My next role was as a customer service manager, where I had 120 people reporting to me. I loved this job, so much responsibility, managing a team of people, learning how to delegate and get results; it inspired me and I loved the interaction with people as well as the entrepreneurial environment. I thrived in this culture. I was promoted several times and I knew I fit into this type of work, as well as the culture of the organization. I left this company only to get new experience and found that in my first marketing agency, where once again the fit was right. As a sales manager of a team, I loved being responsible by being empowered to run things as needed. This was another example of being in the right role with the right leadership and culture. My next move was not as successful; I left agency space to try corporate side. What I found was that I was a lot more entrepreneurial; I liked to move faster and really didn't love the red tape or challenges that came with working with a Fortune 500 company. The irony of this was that people recognized me as being more successful since I had this large organization on my resume, "tier one experience" is what they referred to it as, and in the future it actually opened a lot of doors for me. However, ironically how I remember it as one of the worst places I ever worked, nice people but very demotivating and uninspiring to work there. This is when I knew I had it good in my agency role. I then started on a journey to find the right experience and the right corporate culture for me to be successful and feel a sense of fulfillment. It is a key factor in anyone's happiness to find the right FIT for you, and a more corporate culture is exactly what might work for you, knowing this will help you as you continue to evolve your career and as you look for the right company to call home.

Here are some questions to use as a guide if you are interviewing or researching for your next role in order to help assess cultural fit:

1. What would employees say about what it is like to work here?
2. What kind of company activities do you do for employees?
3. What is the performance development process?
4. How are people rewarded and recognized?
5. What are the career opportunities for me as part of this role or organization?
6. What do you like about working here?
7. Is training and development a part of the organizational culture?
8. What kind of leaders do you have working here?
9. What will I not like about working here?
10. If I were to be successful, what is the plan to help onboard me?
11. How would you explain the culture of the organization?

Chapter Eleven
WELLNESS
The Whole Person Philosophy

We have already chatted on the different parts of your life and how the coaching wheel can help you identify the areas that you would like to work on or how much you value a certain part of your life. Remembering that we never only bring one piece of ourselves to anything. All the pieces add up and show up in different ways. We need to look at ourselves as a whole person made up of many areas that can either make us our best selves or wanting for more. If there is an area that is out of sorts, it can throw off how we are feeling in other areas of our life. We all know what happens when our health is impacted. Even the common cold of flu can drain our energy and make us struggle through our day.

When we can get clear on what parts of our life that are impacting us and work through the clutter, we are free to be whoever we want to be and the very best that we can be.

For me, my starting circle comes down to health and wellness. And when I talk about this part of my circle, it has to be in line before anything else really feels good or right. I never feel like I am at my best if I am not managing this part of my wheel. We all know how important it is to eat right, exercise, and get enough sleep, but do we really? Are we clear on how much this really impacts us in our daily lives? How much it affects our clarity of mind, our energy and vitality, our emotional intelligence and how we react to daily stresses?

I personally believe that your wellness philosophy impacts your whole person. I think it is the greatest gift we give ourselves by first taking care of us and doing the things that we need to do to feel good. The motivation to keep doing the right things is not always easy but the reward at the end is very clear.

When I am not eating well or exercising, I feel a disappointment in myself that even when I try to pretend that it doesn't matter, my clothes still fit, etc., I know deep inside that I am not being my best self. When I stay on top of my game, there is a feeling and a freedom that comes with managing your life and making it your own. It bleeds into everything else that I do. I want to jump up in the morning; and be excited about my life, excited about what is ahead and knowing that I have the energy and focus to do so. Those days when I have that feeling, there is nothing I cannot accomplish; even if things go wrong somehow my mindset still stays strong and positive.

For me, exercise has always been a big part of my life. Sports brought a sense of accomplishment; teamwork and being involved were always an important piece of my identity. When it is not a part of my life, I feel like something is missing. For those who didn't grow up with sports in your life, this may be something you have done as you have gotten older, recognizing that physical activity is just plain good for us. No matter what your sport or activity is, having one is the important thing. Sports can bring social as well as physical wellbeing to your circle and can help you live longer for both reasons. Golf is a great example of this. As some people may say, golf is not really a physical sport, but it can be if you walk the greens and it is social. Spending that much time on a golf course with three other people will automatically help with your social connections. Whatever you have an interest in, it is important to keep this up and make time for it in your life. When you are feeling isolated or lonely, see if you can join a club that helps you to connect both physically and emotionally. It can also reactivate a sense of purpose in your life. As we go through different phases in our lives, we need different things and remembering those things that make you feel good or that you have a passion for can be very uplifting and inspiring.

Regular routine is also very important, as it relates to overall wellness and looking after the whole person. If you do not have some sort of regular routine, it is important to establish one that you can feel good about and make your own. If you like time in the morning to sit and relax, build this into your schedule; it may mean waking up a little earlier but so worth it if you feel more focused and relaxed starting your day. I like time to relax and focus myself on my goals and exercise in the morning. If I have a morning when I get time to do those things, I am off for a good start to a productive day. When I miss this routine, I feel like something is missing all day. I don't have the same energy or focus and I feel a little lost all day long. It is important to listen to your body as well, as there may be some days we just need to rest more than anything else and so also giving yourself the okay to break routine when needed is also very healthy. There have been times in my life when I was so focused on keeping my routine that I exhausted myself trying to keep up the running and exercise each morning. Make sure to check in with yourself on what is working and what isn't and give yourself a break when needed.

By keeping a journal of activities and how you feel each day, this can help you look back to determine where you may be going wrong, what parts need more focus or simply congratulating yourself for getting your exercise in each week. I keep a journal of what I eat each day, when I exercise and what my goals are each week. I then determine how I feel, what needs adjusting, and constantly keep monitoring for myself how I am doing. I have a very strong incentive about feeling good each day. It's less about what I weigh or what size I am but more about how I feel, how much energy I have and if I am feeling optimistic and strong. This also helps with resilience and mindset. I truly believe I feel stronger mentally when I feel stronger physically. And this helps with all of life's ups and downs and to be more resilient when life throws you a curveball.

Before the pandemic hit, I was travelling all over the world for work. I was loving the work I did but it was a very stressful time. I was working over 80 hours a week in a different foreign country every second week and managing against some very tight deadlines and high expectations. Each day I was expected to deliver excellence and this was really wearing on me. I was not sleeping or eating well; there was not time for exercising as the constant demands of a global role was too much.

When the pandemic hit, it was almost a relief that I could no longer travel, and it gave me the opportunity to get back to who I wanted to be. Be more in control over my time and what I ate and getting my exercise in. It reminded me of what was important and how I wanted to live the rest of my life. Those morning routines and getting your exercise in made a huge difference in who I was and how I felt about myself. I lost 15 pounds very quickly once I got back into a regular routine; it wasn't the goal but the output of living my best life.

If you are living truly in your power, which is that combination of finding purpose and using your innate gifts to do something impactful, part of this is feeling good. Having the energy to explore new things, being curious about your life, feeling hopeful about your future. All of these things change as we work on being our best physical selves. The mind and the body are so connected, and when we take care of our physical body our mind comes right along with it. Mindset, as we have discussed, is one of the most powerful tools you have at your disposal and creating the optimal space for us to feel optimism and in control of our lives starts with eating well and exercising. It doesn't matter what moving your body looks like for you; it could be a quick walk around the block, or it may be getting to the gym three times per week. But whatever that is for you, commit to something to make you feel better. Thirty minutes of exercise a day has been proven to support better overall mental and physical health, and although it seems some days so hard to do, it really is about planning and making it a priority. Because my family is also very focused on exercise, I am lucky enough to have equipment in my home and a small gym so that no matter what the weather I have no excuse but to get down there to do something. I have added a TV so if I am feeling lazy at least I can watch TV while I ride the bike or do some sort of exercise. Whatever you need to help you stick to your commitments, build it into your life so that it makes it easier for you to stick to your routine. My preference is to be outside and when the weather is good that is where you will find me. For many years I was a runner until I hurt my knee in a ski accident, and when I was a runner I ran in all weather, rain, snow and very cold temperatures. The thought of not getting my run in was devastating. It was almost like an addiction. For years I struggled to find something that I loved as much as running; now I love to go on long hikes and so whenever I can I get out and do that. Finding something that you love to do, whether it is swimming or golf or tennis. Anything that moves you is an important piece in keeping you motivated to do it. Also finding a buddy or a club to do it with is also helpful; likeminded people always help you to stick to your goal and motivate you to come even when you don't feel like it.

Creating that life for yourself where you are your best self means constantly challenging your ideas and thoughts to push yourself to be the best you can be. My hope for you is that you find this part, as I believe it is one of the most important pieces to help you with everything else in your life. If you get this wellbeing built in and working well, you may be amazed at how everything else comes together too.

Let's brainstorm together some activities you think would like to do and start to think of how you could build a plan to do them. Here are some ideas to get the thoughts flowing:

ACTIVITY	TIMING	WHO TO DO THIS WITH	START DATE
Golf	Spring	choose 3 friends	2021
Basketball	winter	find a team to join	now

Next let's talk about what might need to happen to start eating better or feeling motivated to stay on track.

ACTIVITY	WHO OR WHAT CAN HELP	TIMING
Read some nutritional books		
Meet with a dietician or nutritionist		
Join a club to inspire likeminded thinking		

Even if you just picked one of the ideas you have for yourself from the top, you will be moving in the right direction!

Create

Chapter Twelve

SETTING YOUR GOALS
AND CREATING YOUR ACTION PLAN

Now that you have spent some time reflecting, it is important to do a bit of editing of our thoughts and ideas. It has been great to just let your thinking go where it needs to as part of the first steps of reflecting and dreaming. Now we need to add in the lens of reality. Looking back to all the areas you have explored and identify what is most important, what do you really want to change and why? Then you can start to build a plan as to how to get there. The first exercise I would like you to do is review the main thoughts or ideas from each chapter. As you look at what most resonated with you, use the One Wild and Precious Life Model to help you sort through what you want to think about doing now versus later. After doing this I would like you to write your WHY statement, as this will guide the rest of the process. Your why should help you have the motivation and courage to start to build your plan. If your why is not strong enough, you may need to do further work so that you feel it so strongly in your soul that you have to make the changes. Spend some time crafting your why by letting the writing flow. Write up to two paragraphs, then try to get it down to one or two sentences. The more concise your why, the more powerful it can be. The objective of this section is also to help you set your goals and then work on the tactics to get there. You can have a large goal like "changing my career" and then we will need to plan for specific tools to break this goal down into individual pieces to determine what needs to happen when. At this point we also need to think about what may be holding us back. What obstacles or beliefs do you have that you need to recognize as part of this process that you may need to overcome? What needs to happen to make you really feel that you can make these goals happen? Some limiting beliefs can be things like "I am too old," "I don't have enough money," "It will never work," "I don't have the time right now." You may need to challenge yourself on some of these beliefs, figure out why they are rising up for you and determining what is the truth and what needs to happen to help manage them. We also may have fears about making this change; this is a powerful piece and sometimes when we break a goal apart into smaller pieces, we can see how the fear can go away. The right plan or process to get there can alleviate the fear or caution you may have. For example, when I wanted to shift my career to learning and coaching, I had a fear of not getting paid to do the work I wanted to do. By doing some research on others in the field, I was able to alleviate that fear as others were out there making a good living from coaching. Also wanting to go back to school when we did not have a lot of money or time was a real obstacle, but by breaking my goal into a 5-year plan I was able to accomplish this by spending small amounts each year on courses that finally led up to me finishing my masters of education. Yes, it took 5 years, but I knew what my long-term goal was and so many smaller goals were made to build up to my final objective. Also, very important was the support that was needed for me to finish my goal. I had two small children and my husband and I both worked full time. I needed him to agree to help with the kids and other household duties so that I could sneak away for classes and have time for homework. I am lucky that I had this wonderful support and someone who believed in my goals no matter how much sacrifice was needed. Another reason why one of our goals in life is to ensure we are with the right people, people who understand you and get your WHY. To live your best life, you will need to have some of these people to not only support the day-to-day but to encourage you and keep you going in the hard days. When I was about halfway through my masters, it was getting hard for me and my husband to keep it going. We were tired and school was just another thing that I had on my plate. We had a friend over for dinner one weekend and he asked how my masters was going. I shared how I was feeling and that I might just give it up. His reaction had a profound effect on me; he said, "You cannot do that; you started this for a reason and unless your reason has changed you will always regret that decision." It was like a lightning bolt. He was right, how could I just give up my goal? It was what was giving me hope to have a career where I really felt fulfilled. Without it I would have really felt a disappointment in myself for not pushing through and getting to the goal I was so passionate about. We need to feel hope, we need to have something to look forward to, to help us keep a positive outlook on our lives. Knowing that you can work on something and make a true difference in your life is an empowering feeling and will help you in other facets of your life. If you think about what you would want for your children or nieces or nephews, do you not want them to fly as high as they can? Do you not want them to create a life that makes them happy? Then why wouldn't you want this for yourself! I am so grateful for my family and friends who supported me and continued to help keep me inspired to meet my goal. Otherwise, this book would have never been written.

ONE WILD AND PRECIOUS LIFE MODEL

WHAT ARE YOUR TAKEAWAYS FROM EACH CHAPTER OF THIS BOOK?

Chapter One:_____

Chapter Two:_____

Chapter Three: _____

Chapter Four: _____

Chapter Five: _____

Chapter Six: _____

Chapter Seven: _____

Chapter Eight: _____

Chapter Nine: _____

Chapter Ten: _____

Chapter Eleven: _____

MY WHY STATEMENT IS: (try to write it in two paragraphs and then in two sentences)

_____

_____

_____

_____

_____

_____

_____

_____

_____

_____

_____

_____

_____

_____

_____

_____

SETTING YOUR GOALS

When we set goals, we need to create both long-term and short-term goals. For example, if your goal is to write a book, you would set the long-term goal by stating a year for it to be completed, then the next step is to create short-term goals to meet this goal. For example, write three chapters by May. Goals need to be *SMART,* specific, measurable, achievable, relevant and timely. Without the details around the goal, it will not be tangible enough to put into reality. Long-term and high-level goals can be more visionary, but when we get to short-term goals we need to create the practical elements.

IDENTIFY YOUR LONG-TERM GOALS AND GIVE A TIMELINE TO EACH: 10 YEARS, 5 YEARS, 2 YEARS.

TOPIC   TIMING

1.

2.

3.

4.

5.

6.

Coming out of this exercise, what are your top three goals to create your best life in the short term that you can set some specific next steps and timelines on?

TOPIC	TIMELINE
1.	
2.	
3.	

Now that we have set some goals, we need to determine what some of the obstacles or barriers may be in order to make these goals come true. For each goal, please write the obstacle and the support you will need to make this goal work for you. Be realistic here, and sometimes we have to rework our goals in a way that makes them practical.

GOAL	OBSTACLE	SUPPORT NEEDED
1 Write a book	time to write	daily book support group
2		
3		

BELIEVING

The biggest part of meeting our goals is believing that we can. This can be the biggest obstacle for us to see the vision come true. When you think about this life change, what does it look like for you? Can you visualize it, how are you feeling now that it is done, how is your life different now that you met the goal? The power of visualization and really seeing yourself getting to the end is sometimes the reason it can work. For example, if you have ever wanted to lose weight, visualizing yourself in that bikini on a beach, or being able to run half-marathons because you are in such great shape. All of these are powerful messages for our brain, and when our brain believes we are more apt to make it happen.

Research has shown that there is a strong scientific basis for how and why visualization works. It is a well-known fact that we stimulate the same brain regions when we visualize an action and when we actually perform that same action. (Sept. 13, 2013, voler.com)

HOW TO VISUALIZE

Simply put, visualization starts with establishing a goal, then imagining accomplishing that goal in detail, focusing on it over the long term. Many visualization techniques exist, and anyone can practice one or many of them to help achieve their goals.

A basic technique involves sitting with eyes closed while imagining yourself achieving a specific dream in as much detail as possible. While doing so, envision the goal as though you have already achieved it. You can set aside a little time each day or several days a week to integrate this practice into your routine.

VISION BOARDS

Many also swear by this visualization technique in which a person cuts out pictures from magazines and newspapers representing their goals before creating a collage of pictures showcasing what they would like to achieve.

AFFIRMATIONS

Daily affirmations help build confidence and lay out goals clearly. Choose positive affirmations that lift you up and break barriers obstructing you from the life you want to lead. For example, someone who feels unworthy of love can repeat to themselves each morning, "I love myself. My family and friends love me. I deserve love."

In the end, if you do not strongly believe that the goal is achievable it will not work. Just like our why, we need to feel it in our gut, know that it is something we really want to do; it needs to link strongly with your why to not only motivate you but also keep you believing. When I have struggled in the past, I have relied on friends who can give me the outside view of the goal I am setting. For example, for many years I wanted to run my own business but I had a base belief that I would not be successful, it wouldn't work. I surrounded myself with people who were already doing it and learned from them on how they made their businesses work. This gave me the confidence to try and go out on my own, but without the strong belief that I could do it and the connection back to my fundamental why it would not have worked.

ACCOUNTABILITY

In coaching, accountability is one of the strongest factors in success. Knowing you have someone who is supporting you on your journey and who helps you set milestones helps us to stay on track. After any training session that I deliver, I ask the audience to find an accountability partner for any of the goals they might have created. Having someone check in on you, on your goal is one of the most powerful things to help remind you of your why and have success.

We also can create our own accountability to ourselves. If we have a regular morning routine where we review our daily goals and plan, and journal how we are feeling, this is a powerful way to keep us focused on the things we want to accomplish. Studies have shown that people wanting to lose weight are more successful when they write down what they eat. It helps to keep them accountable to the calories. Some people meditate and this is also a great way to keep you body and mind in focus on what is important. I tend to put my vision board up and also hang reminders in my office to remind myself of what and who I want to do and be. Each year when I do my business planning, I hang a whiteboard with all the pieces I want to accomplish for my business. Almost everything I post up comes true. I truly believe it is because I can't miss it each day hanging as a reminder of what I strategically took time to think through and link to my why. It helps me to reflect often on the "Oh yeah, that's right, how am I getting this done?" or "How am I getting closer to that goal?" Accountability can be very personal, so I encourage you to find something that will work for you. It doesn't matter what it is, as long as you build it into your life with consistency. *The discipline needs to be there when the motivation goes away.*

WHAT DO YOU NEED TO DO TO BELIEVE...?

CLOSING

My hope is that you have found value in working through the many activities and reflection points in this book and that you were able to design your long-term and short-term goals that clearly link back to your why. The One Wild and Precious Life model is a good reminder to utilize all of the facets in your life and remembering how these unique pieces are yours to own and use to their full advantage. You deserve to live the life that best utilizes who you are and that will bring you the greatest happiness. You have this in your control, and only you can make this happen for yourself. "Nobody ever lived a meaningful life by aiming to be like everyone else." Use your innate gifts to create the life that you deserve, and enjoy your one wild and precious life!

CPSIA information can be obtained
at www.ICGtesting.com
Printed in the USA
LVHW081338150721
692800LV00010B/294